Growing in Ministry

Using Critical Incident Analysis in Pastoral Care

Charles Chadwick

Priest-in-Charge of Stokenchurch and Ibstone
Formerly Assistant Director of the
Chiltern Christian Training Programme

Phillip Tovey

Training Officer, Diocese of Oxford

GROVE BOOKS LIMITED
RIDLEY HALL RD CAMBRIDGE CB3 9HU

Contents

Acknowledgements

We would like to thank members of the congregation at Saint Peter and Saint Paul, Stokenchurch for their help in data collecting, various groups of people in ministry in the Diocese of Oxford, and the Grove Pastoral Group for their encouragement and in particular Rev Roger Walton, Canon Gordon Oliver, and Rev Dr Gavin Wakefield.

Know Yourself

Our greatest protection is self-knowledge, and to avoid the delusion that we are seeing ourselves when we are in reality looking at something else.

Gregory of Nyssa

The Cover Illustration is by Peter Ashton

Copyright © Charles Chadwick and Phillip Tovey 2000

First Impression December 2000
ISSN 0144-171X
ISBN 1 85174 451 7

1

A Real Story: A Funny Thing Happened...

Story 1

Our church was having a stewardship campaign and I was asked to be one of the visitors. My neighbour is 80 and a regular church attender and on the electoral roll. Her son was building my new conservatory and does not go to church.

He came in very angry: 'Have you seen this letter? They are trying to squeeze money out of my old mum, who is a pensioner.' 'Yes, we are having a stewardship campaign.' 'How dare they do this,' he replied, 'the church has lots of money. It's all because the church lost all that money a few years ago and now they expect my mum to pay for their mistakes. Anyway there is loads of money in the Vatican, why don't they sell something. Look at this they are insisting that my mum pay more.' He waved the letter at me. 'We do need more money in our local church to pay...' I tried to explain calmly, even if by now I was feeling a bit ruffled, but he shouted: 'So you support demanding money off old ladies. She is very upset. Is that what the church is about—getting money off the elderly?' 'We're not demanding...' 'Look what it says, "you should seriously consider giving 5% to the church and 5% to charity."' I replied: 'Well the Bible...' 'Don't give me the Bible; you are all a bunch of money-grabbing hypocrites. Demanding money from 80-year-old pensioners is immoral. Call yourself a Christian? Do your own conservatory. I'm so angry that I will have nothing to do with you.' He stomped out.

I was really unhappy about this. Even after talking it over with my spouse I could not get it out of my mind. I looked again at the letter (which the Vicar had written) and thought it could have been a little less direct. I mentioned the incident to the Vicar at the church door on Sunday but this was not the right time. At the stewardship visitors meeting I mentioned it again, but the leader, a Reader, said this was only one incident and that the rest of it was going well and people had been responding. So I felt that there was nothing I could do.

In a training day for a pastoral care course we were asked to reflect on an incident and I raised this in a small group. I explained the situation and my feelings (still a bit raw). We were encouraged to help one another, look at issues, and relate them to the Bible. I heard from others about difficult situations that they had experienced and I did not feel quite so bad. We thought about having to take responsibility for the actions of others, the Vicar's letter, in the body of Christ. We thought a bit about Paul being flogged for Christ's sake (it had felt like a flogging). We also prayed a bit and were encouraged to look at what we might do next time or what future help we might need. I knew that I hate conflict and wondered how to 'burst the bubble' in this situation. I also saw that this was probably a 'no win' situation. All this helped me not to feel so bad about the event and I saw that if you take on the role of stewardship visitor, you sometimes get flack for doing this. Maybe next time I will not be naïve about this possibility.

This is a real story and similar stories could be repeated. But what if there had been no pastoral course? It could have meant that there was no development and learning from this painful event. It would have been easy to give up and withdraw. But that would not have solved the problem nor led to growth. It would have been to become a victim rather than to learn from the incident. This booklet is all about how to learn from such experiences and go forward in Christian discipleship. It will look at a number of examples of learning from incidents and work through some methods. It will look at the place of pastoral groups and how looking at critical incidents can be used in mutual support and development. It will relate pastoral incidents to theological reflection (although this booklet is not primarily about theological reflection). But first it will look at Scripture and reflect on some of the life-stories to be found in the Bible.

2

Critical Incidents and Scripture

Story 2

I had taken up a job in agriculture away from home because I had got into serious trouble while I was younger and feared for my safety. While working in the fields I saw something really odd in the distance and went to investigate. When I arrived, God spoke to me and told me to return home and become the leader of my community. I felt amazed that God should choose me as leader not least because I had failed to convince people in the past of my position as leader. (I have to ask myself who chose me then? Was I rather appointing myself? Was I trusting in my authority because of my adopted family background?) I was awestruck. I was actually talking to God. I was worried too about my safety and my ability to do the job. I tried to talk myself out of this post. But God was not having that. He gave me my brother to help me. I thus gave up farming and became a preacher. Now I see that I had previously put myself forward out of my own ambition and not thought about God much at all. I reckoned that I had all the answers—such is the presumption of youth. When God did speak, I was forced to think about things completely afresh and give up my own ambitions and plans. I now see that God has his own timing and when he says jump you have to jump. I also see the futility of trying to avoid God's call. He is *very* persistent! With further insight I was really glad to have my brother with me and he gave me support in some of the difficult times, although his judgment was sometimes way out, and nearly wrecked everything at one point.

4

This is the story of Moses written in the format of the first story. As we cannot interview Moses, some imagination is required to recast the story. In fact, imagination is essential in this approach as we will see later. Examples of learning from experience are frequent in the Scriptures. Other Old Testament examples include that of Abraham and Isaac in Genesis 22, where Abraham learns what it means to have complete trust in God, and Joseph's reassurance of his brothers after Jacob's death in Genesis 50, where Joseph sees God's hand in the cruel episodes of his life. Often, as with Moses, there is a lot more learning to be done, and the stories go on to develop this theme in a person's life. But through this we can often see that the people involved are just as fallible as we are, and sometimes they need to learn something more than once. Of course, there are plenty of instances where people seem unable or unwilling to learn, such as Aaron and the people creating the golden calf despite the experience of Exodus, or the repeated cycle of obedience and disobedience by the people of Israel, as depicted in the book of Judges.

It is our belief that the examples of learning by experience and reflection found in the Bible indicate the validity of this approach in the twenty-first century. Indeed such stories, even allowing for the differences in times and culture between the world of the Bible and the world of today, provide appropriate examples of reflection and learning on which we can build.

As the story of Moses shows, reflection on experience can be a sign of wisdom and maturity. It is in and through human experience that God works. One of the roots of this can be seen in the wisdom literature in the Old Testament. As John Goldingay has observed, 'Wisdom is…[a] pragmatic approach to life…[it] is experience centred,' it seeks to 'do theology on the basis of how everyday life actually is.'[1] It is by reflecting on critical incidents that we can be more open to hearing God speak to us and so achieve a knowledge of both God and ourselves.

Like the Old Testament, the New Testament has examples of people learning from their experiences.

Story 3

My life as a fisherman seemed constant and routine—dealing with the weather, searching out the fish, maintaining the boat, working in a business partnership—all to keep going and to provide for me and my family. Then word began to spread of the new teacher from Nazareth. We'd heard about such folk before. Most of them did not really have much about them. Anyway, this new man made his home in our town. One day, after we'd had a long fruitless night's work, he came down to the waterside and asked to borrow my boat. He wanted to use it to teach from. I let him use it and we sat back and listened. He wasn't centred on himself but God. He spoke of God's kingdom in a way that we could appreciate. When he'd finished he suggested we put the nets out again. A bit of me wasn't too impressed by this, I must say. What could he know about fishing? But we had a go, and to our

---

1   J Goldingay, *Theological Diversity and the Authority of the Old Testament* (Grand Rapids: Eerdmans, 1987) pp 207, 211.

amazement the nets were soon full to breaking point. Just who was this person? How did he know where the fish were? I did not know the answers but I sensed something of God in what he had spoken of, and in what had happened that morning. I felt compelled to follow him and find out more.

In this story Peter makes himself available to Jesus. He hears his word. He sees the deed. He allows all of this to make an impact on him. He reflects by asking himself questions. And from all of that he makes a response. Indeed, a number of times Jesus asks his disciples questions that show he expected them to learn from their experiences. In Mark 8.14–21 he questions their understanding of the feeding miracles and this leads to the crucial questions: 'Who do people say I am?' 'Who do you say I am?' Jesus expected his disciples to learn from experience.

Story 4

I had been a faithful missionary for the gospel yet I found my eyesight was failing. I had to get other people to write my letters for me. Since my living as a tent-maker also relied on my being able to see clearly, all of this was pretty frightening. I had been so zealous for the Lord Jesus Christ. Why was this happening to me after all I'd done for the gospel? Would not it be better if I were fully fit? Then I could do so much more for God. Three times I asked God to relieve me of my trouble. I spent time thinking about all of this in the light of the Scriptures. I remembered the story of Elijah when he was at a very low ebb. Then he had encountered God on the mountain. I reflected that maybe, like Elijah, I need to learn that God has a bigger plan than just me. I recalled the story of Naaman and that God can and does heal, but he does not always. And then I thought of a whole range of characters that God had used, and that God uses people in many different ways according to his purposes and not ours. In and through all of this the Spirit spoke to me. He gave me courage to keep going. My feelings of discontent and unhappiness were changed for feelings of acceptance and contentment that the power of Christ could and would work in and through my affliction.

In this version of Paul's 'grace being sufficient in weakness' (2 Cor 12) we have illustrated the place that Scripture takes in a process of learning from a critical incident, in this case illness. It is not just that learning from experience happens in Scripture, or that it was something that Jesus expected of his disciples. Scripture takes a part in the process of learning as our story and Scripture interact.

In all the stories in this chapter we have seen an incident, a reflection on the incident (usually in the form of questioning about the situation and of the people involved in it) and subsequent action in the form of a change in behaviour. It is only after reflecting on an encounter with God that people are able properly to move on. We will see more of this as we proceed through the booklet.

We believe that the Bible is an essential component in the whole process of being able to learn from experience. It helps avoid the trap of thinking merely in terms of this world and its values. It places our experiences within the framework of the Christian story, which provides us with examples and reference points to draw upon. Using the Bible in this work reminds us that it is not our experiences which should be at the centre. Rather we need to bring our experiences to the Christian story for clarification, discernment, and guidance in their interpretation. We need to remember that 'the hard facts of life, which knock some of the nonsense out of us, are *God's* facts and his appointed school of character: they are not alternatives to his grace but means of it; for everything *is* of grace, from the power to know to the power to obey.'[2] We will look further at the use of the Bible in reflection later on, but next we examine how to identify an incident.

3

Identifying an Incident

In order to make good use of the technique which we are outlining in this booklet, it is important to have an appropriate definition of the term 'critical incident.' One needs to be clear that what makes it critical is that it is an event, or series of events, which lie outside one's normal range of usual experiences. It is not a sense of crisis which makes it critical. It is the response it produces. A critical incident is one which produces an emotional reaction in the person who experiences it. It makes an impact. It makes one think. It suggests that there is more to a situation than meets the eye. It raises questions.[3]

Incidents suitable for analysis and reflection can and should be drawn from a wide range of experiences, both positive and negative—those occasions which make us want to rejoice and those which make us want to weep. To select either all positive or all negative incidents can limit the benefits gained from analysis and reflection. An undue emphasis on positive incidents can result in a dearth of questioning about conduct, usual ways of thinking, and viewing the world. An excessive stress on negative incidents has the potential to lower self-esteem and our sense of competence and confidence. An appropriate balance needs to be struck. One of the ways of doing this is to pair incidents and work at a successful incident and a less successful incident together. Stephen Brookfield commends describing the successful event first because dealing with one's successes is much less threatening than having to face one's failures.[4] Yet describing our negative incidents can teach us more about ourselves and give a fuller picture of the assumptions and values which underlie our thoughts and actions.

---

2   D Kidner, *Proverbs* (London: IVP, 1964, 1974) p 35.
3   See P Ballard and J Pritchard, *Practical Theology in Action* (London: SPCK, 1996) p 94.
4   See, S Brookfield in J Mezirow and Associates, *Fostering Critical Reflection in Adulthood* (San Francisco: Jossey-Bass Publishers, 1990) pp 177–193.

Story 5

At the monthly meeting of the Home Visitors' Team I described an incident which had happened to me in recent weeks. I have always found it something of a trial to visit one particular person. In truth I dread going there. It is always the same old story. She goes on and on about how much better things were in the past. So last week, just as she as getting under way, I asked her, 'Please can you show me something from your past?' Off she went and came back with a dusty box full of papers. After much searching she found a certificate showing she had passed the eleven-plus exam well over fifty years ago. 'So did you enjoy your time at Grammar School?' I asked. 'Oh I never made it, my family couldn't afford the uniform,' came the quiet reply. And then out it all came: the sense of disappointment, of not being good enough, of letting oneself down, of having reached the heights already at the age of eleven. 'How do you feel about it all now?' I asked. 'Well, dear, you're the first person I've ever told. Thank you.'

I spoke to the team of how, in a strange way, I felt that I had really helped the person address something deeply-rooted in her past, painful as it had been. On being asked what made me ask to be shown something I reflected back that there had been two factors. One was a desire not to have to hear the same old story again. The other was just how often people in the Bible have to learn to let things go if they are ever to move on. Abraham leaving Haran, Jacob leaving his family, and the disciples leaving their occupations, were three such examples. Discussion with other members of the team made me think how all of us can hold on to experiences throughout our lives, and how being the right person at the right time can enable people to at least address such experiences, if not resolve them.

This story illustrates that on occasions a critical incident can make an impression or impact in different ways at different times with different people. The first incident had happened more than fifty years ago, but had never been articulated and reflected upon. It truly was unfinished business. Rooted in the same incident is the Home Visitor's reflection, which had three aspects to it. It was both *theological*, in drawing on the Christian story, *pastoral*, in the discussion of an approach to a particular situation, and *personal*, by individual reflection.

Story 6

Last week, I called at a home where I am always warmly welcomed. I enjoy going to visit this person. The door opened as usual and I was told, 'I'm sorry but it's not convenient to see you today. The painter's calling to give me a quote for the guttering,' and the door was shut. I felt pretty hurt and rejected by this. 'Surely my visit is more important than the painter's. I've worked really hard to make time to come here today,' I thought as I left the property. I was inclined just to put it out of my mind or even not visit this person again. After all, many people said how good and conscientious I was at pastoral work. Reflecting on this incident with members of our Pastoral Team helped me to reconsider my reaction. What had made me so upset? Who might have been benefiting most from my visits? I resolved to spend time thinking about my assumptions about being a Pastoral Visitor, not least in terms of my own wants and needs. I came to see that in visiting I had a need to be wanted, that this was a shadow side to my helping others and that I had felt rejected because this person was not grateful for my helping.[5] I had to spend time in prayer to re-centre my thoughts and feelings and check through what I was doing. In the end this gave me a greater sense of calling and a more realistic view of ministry.

The range of stories used so far have illustrated that while incidents can have an element of crisis within them, crisis is not an essential component of a critical incident. Rather it is that element which makes us stop and think, and which make us wonder what is going on here. A useful skill to develop is that of journalling and recording, to which we will return. A further key skill is learning how to identify which incidents should be examined. One potential danger is that one tries to record everything in a journal so that what should be a liberating task becomes an onerous duty. Appropriate selectivity is the key. Praying for the gift of discernment is a prerequisite for this work as is commitment to allowing time for it. Often further reflection can be beneficial. Following from story 6 the Visitor could, after a period of say, three months, review her or his pattern and style of visiting. This could enable further learning to take place. This is particularly important in that it is often over a period of time that one can begin to identify one's traits, one's preferred style of working and one's assumptions.

Of course, not all incidents have a distinct beginning and conclusion. For Peter and Paul, working out the implications of their calling took their whole lifetime. But incidents which are concluded, such as a discrete piece of work similar to that outlined in story 1, have the potential to result in changed perceptions and actions in the short term. Concluded incidents can be more straightforward to reflect upon than those which are still ongoing. This, of course, raises the question of when is an incident concluded. A simple answer is: when an incident raises no more questions. While this may appear to be a counsel of perfection, it is generally easier to maintain an appropriate level of distance and detachment from something which has ended, rather than something which is ongoing. There is a greater potential for reflection, and so new understanding and the possibility of growth, in things which are finished.

The great value of critical incident analysis and reflection lies in its being grounded in one's own data, and one's own experiences. We now turn to a format for journalling and reflecting on critical incidents which will assist in recording and will prevent an inappropriate element of subjectivity such that reflection is not undertaken from a position of faith.

---

5   For shadow side see, M Goldsmith, *Knowing Me –Knowing God* (London: Triangle, 1994) pp 81–83.

4
Learning from an Incident

Learning from mistakes (and successes) in life is very important. If you were training pilots, it would be very important to learn the reasons for any accidents, so that their recurrence could be avoided. The reasons might include inappropriate training, such as their not receiving enough information before you let them in the air, or simple things like the layout of the cockpit. Analysis of incidents involving American Air Force pilot training in the Second World War is in fact the origin of the technique which we are outlining in this book.[6] It was then used in industrial production, and in commerce. Latterly, its merits have become recognized in the nursing and teaching professions.[7] The development of variations in method from the original technique has led to a wider and increasingly fruitful application of the approach.

The following is a method used in the Dioceses of Canterbury and Rochester and slightly adapted here:[8]

Critical Incidents: Method 1

1. Select an incident from your journal or from recent experience.
2. Write this up as a log (or story) mentioning:
   - When and where things happened?
   - Who was involved?
   - What happened?
   - What you were thinking, doing and feeling?
   - What it seemed others were thinking, doing and feeling?
3. List all the questions that come into your mind. It is important to ask why.
4. Select some of the questions to look at more deeply.
5. Explore these looking at insights and research from the Bible, theology and contemporary approaches.
6. Identify alternative ways of acting and thinking either to improve your ministry or give you confidence that your present approach is right.

---

6 J C Flanagan, 'The Critical Incident Technique' *Psychological Bulletin*, (1954, 51, 4) pp 327–358.
7 See D F S Cormack, 'The Critical Incident Technique' in D F S Cormack, *The Research Process in Nursing* (Oxford: Blackwell, 1984, 1991, 1996) pp 266–274; D Tripp, *Critical Incidents in Teaching, Developing Professional Judgment* (London: Routledge, 1994).
8 Diocese of Canterbury and Diocese of Rochester, *Kent Post Ordination Handbook 1999-2000* (1999).

This can then be worked through and used as the following example demonstrates.

Story 7
1. This event happened a few years ago but is significant in changing my views.
2. A new family came to the communion service in church on Sunday. It was their first visit.
   - Dad brought his 5 year-old son up to the front. Mum stayed with the baby in the seat (about 5 rows behind).
   - When the Vicar gave the boy 'a blessing,' the lad turned round and said very loudly 'that man did not give me any bread.'
   - There seemed to be some embarrassment by the Vicar (who flushed slightly) and the congregation (slight titters). Dad told him to be quiet.
   - I too felt embarrassed.
3. Lots of questions came into my mind—about welcoming new families, worries that this might drive them away, about who should be allowed to receive communion, and about the understanding of faith for this boy. I also imagined what the church would be like if all the children received communion.
4. I wanted to look more deeply into the questions around children and communion, as I knew that this was being discussed in the churches.
5. I thought again about the verses on baptism in the Scriptures that emphasize that once you are baptized you are a full part of the church. I remember the words at the baptismal service 'we are members together of the body of Christ.' I looked into where the present practice of making confirmation as a gateway to communion came from, noting that the Roman Catholics do not do this. I read a report from Culham, which looked at the effects on children of receiving communion from an early age, particularly at the numbers who stay during the teenage years.
6. All of this made me change my mind from being happy with the contemporary practice of our church to wanting a change in policy. So I asked if the church council could discuss the issue, to see if baptized children might be admitted to communion (the result of that is another story).

The analysis of this event has carefully followed the numbering of the method, as adapted from the Kent dioceses, to show a worked example. It entailed some new observation, the practice of the nearby Roman Catholic Church, with whom we had very friendly relationships. It also required some study, grabbing a copy of *Anglican Worship Today* and a report from a local institution which had been reviewed in the diocesan newspaper. The results were not simple. While one mind was changed this was not the effect on all the people, and it did not lead to a change in the local church's policy. But it has convinced this one person about the rightness of a change towards the inclusion of baptized children in communion.

This illustrates how quite brief incidents can stick in the mind and lead to a change of view. It also shows a simple method of 'theological reflection,' which is about the way theology is related to practice when beginning with a life experience.[9]

The next example in this chapter uses a slightly different method one which we have used in a number of workshops in the Diocese of Oxford. It uses two worksheets set out as A4 pages.

Critical Incidents: Method 2, Part 1: The Incident

Take a significant event for you and answer the following questions about it. The event may be either good or bad.

Approximate date_____(month)_____(year)

Good   1   2   3   4   5   6   Bad

1. Describe the events that happened.
2. What were your feelings at the time?
3. What were your immediate reactions and judgments?

This can be illustrated by the following as a worked example for this method.

Story 8, Part 1: The Incident

The event centres on a prayer partnership that had been going on for the last 6 months. I would rate this as a 1 on a scale of 1–6, because I found it very helpful.
1. A while a go I was struggling as a Christian at work. There were a number of people at church who did a similar job and we had all talked a bit about our struggles over coffee at church. I remembered a prayer partnership I had when I was a 20-something and suggested to a friend that we might make a similar partnership over the next few months. We met for 6 months and then had a chat about it. So I am looking from the perspective of the review we had together.
2. My feelings had changed over the period of meeting. At first I was both worried about my job (taking up a set of new responsibilities) and of asking to pray together (would I be seen as odd?). I was relieved when the other person responded with some enthusiasm. After 6 months I am delighted as to how well it has gone. I feel that God had blessed us, I am more confident at work and I have had someone to talk to and pray with through this period.
3. My judgment is that these meetings have been very valuable.

---

9   P O'Connell Killen and J de Beer, *The Art of Theological Reflection* (New York: Crossroad, 1996); W Carr, *Handbook of Pastoral Studies* (London: SPCK, 1997) pp 113–133.

The second part of the process is to reflect theologically on the event, which is the second page of questions:

Critical Incidents: Method 2, Part 2: Reflecting on the Incident

Ask yourself:
1. What does this remind you of in the Scriptures?
2. What do you think God might be saying to you through this?
3. What does it tell you about yourself?
   - Your strengths and weaknesses?
   - Your values and assumptions that you live on?
4. What new learning might you need from this?
5. What might you do differently next time?
6. How do you look at the incident now?

My reflection on the incident was as follows.

Story 8, Part 2: Reflecting on the Incident
1. There are lots of Scriptures that encourage us to pray together. This includes the example in Acts of a powerful prayer meeting. I also thought of Paul's image of the body and how we can work together to help one another.
2. I think God is saying that this has been a part of his blessing to me and that I need to name that.
3. I know that I am quite shy and that it is quite a step for me to initiate a prayer partnership. However, I now see that I can do that and it might actually be good. I see too that I do value prayer (more perhaps than I suspected I did).
4. I would like to learn about different ways of praying and how we might enrich our partnership by 'going deeper' than our present practice of sharing and intercession.
5. Next time I think we might include some celebration at the end, not just a review but also the marking of the value this has been to both of us. I tried to imagine simple ways of doing this.
6. I now look back at the incident as one of the points where God has blessed me in my life. It is important to give thanks back to God for this goodness.

This worked example was deliberately of something good. You do not have to look only at the major crises. Indeed it is important to look at the good events, as we can learn from success. It is also not very long in the analysis. In your analysis you need to focus on the heart of the incident and not be distracted by irrelevant details. This method tries to unearth some of the more hidden assumptions.[10] The example says 'I...value prayer (more than I suspect I did).' This would be a point

---

10   See, S Brookfield, *Developing Critical Thinkers* (San Francisco: Jossey-Bass Publishers, 1987).

for further reflection as there is something here about hidden values and their working out in one person's life. The sixth question encourages reflection on the reflection, something that helps lead to wisdom through growing insight.

This chapter has looked at two methods of learning from an incident. Both use the same underlying approach of collecting information about our own behaviour (values, feelings and actions) and then using this to help us think more deeply about what has happened. The purpose of doing this is to see how we might learn and grow from these experiences, not least in identifying God at work in our lives. The approach is slightly different from the model on which some operate, which is to find out what the Bible says and apply it. It relies more on dynamic interaction between experience and Scripture. This can be done without prejudicing the authority of God's word. It also tries to avoid a pitfall in 'find out and apply' of making the assumption that we *are* always applying Scripture. Sometimes our actions betray us.

The first method in this chapter mentioned journals and story 8 involved a review process. This leads us on to look at a number of important skills that help us to learn from experience, journals—sharing and helping others share—which will be examined in the next chapter.

5
Using Journals and Sharing with Someone

Learning from life is not necessarily a solitary activity. Indeed, it is our conviction that sharing with someone is essential in the process of reflection. Journalling has a long history in autobiography, spirituality, and is increasingly being used to provide evidence of learning. The event recorded in the journal can be the basis for a discussion with someone else. Journalling and good sharing are thus skills that can significantly help in the process of learning from experience.[11]

Journals

Some events stick in the mind; others, while crucial, begin to fade with the flow of life. Journals can be a way of keeping a record of events to be used to help the memory in the process of reflection. There are a number of ways of using journals; one is explained here.[12]

At times both of us have kept journals in a process of reflective learning. From that we have developed a set of simple ground-rules:

1. Keeping a journal is a very helpful discipline in capturing experience that will enrich your learning.
2. The journal is a confidential document. No-one may see it without your permission.
3. You may, however, wish to quote bits when you look at an incident (particularly if you are writing it down). You may wish to use your journal to write out your analysis of events.
4. You may change names for reasons of confidentiality when you are sharing with someone else.
5. What do you put in it?
   - Jottings of events
   - Evaluations of activities
   - Snippets of key conversations
   - Ideas that strike you when reading or listening
   - Thoughts about anything
   - Plans for future activity
   - Poems/prayers you write

11   See Roger Pooley, *Spiritual Autobiography* (Grove Spirituality Booklet S 4)
12   See also, T Ghaye and S Lillyman, *Learning Journals and Critical Incidents: Reflective Practice for Health Care Professionals* (Dinton: Mark Allen Publishing Limited, 1997).

6. Try writing the journal this way. In an exercise book use both pages thus:

Left Page On this page make jottings as in 5 above	*Right page* Use this page to review the left side (monthly) and write down your further reflections.

If we look back at story 3, the jottings in the left page of the journal may have been:

Story 7, Journal Extract
Sunday 12 August New family come to church. At communion when boy is blessed, he turns round to mum and says loudly 'That man did not give me any bread.' Quite a bit of embarrassment. Think about this more.

You may wish to write up a lot more. But this is enough to capture the event, provided that later it enables you to recall the incident in greater depth. The page may have continued with other comments from other events in that week. Then once a month on looking back at what has happened you revisit these few lines and take notice of your comment 'Think about this more.' On the right hand side of the journal you might have worked through the first method of chapter 4. This might then look like story 8 as written in that chapter.

If we look at story 8, which covers a number of events, you might have in the left hand page the following sorts of entry.

Story 8, Journal Extract 1
   February 2 Worried about new responsibilities in job. What can I do? How about meeting someone to pray? B for example.
   February 20 Plucked up courage to ask B to pray monthly with me, who to my surprise said yes!!
   March 2 Met for first time. Felt good and yet unsure. Began to talk about things and pray.
   April 6 Really got sharing and praying. Felt a lot better. Found out B has similar worries.
   May 4 Somehow not so real today. Perhaps we were too polite and not real enough.
   June 8 Yes, got back to real issues. Felt much more encouraged.
   July 8 Can't meet in August B suggested a review in September 6 months already.
   September 7 Looking back thought this had been really good. Thank you God.

These sort of jottings would be included in among other events, such as the incident in story 7 on Sunday 12 August. The example above collects them together. The initial of the other person has been used to illustrate one way of keeping some bits private, in this case to do with keeping confidentiality in a publication. There may have been other comments in June 8 that you might not have wanted to reveal, and not doing so is fine when reporting back. At the point of review B suggested doing a SWOT analysis.[13] This went on one of the right hand pages. The SWOT analysis divides the page into four sections—strengths, weaknesses, opportunities and threats. Thus the journal divided up a right hand page in that way and had the following jottings:

Story 8, Journal Extract 2

Strengths	Weaknesses
Overcame shyness	Unsure beginning
B's openness	Not real all the time
Sharing my worries	Finding a quiet place
Growing friendship	
Opportunities	Threats
A prayer partner	Pressure of time
To be honest with someone	Other agendas taking over
Reviewing what happened	Holidays

Under that, on the same page, was written:

Story 8 Journal extract 3

Looking back this was a really helpful thing to do that came at an important time in my life. I thank God that this has been so fruitful.

This sort of reflection can then be the basis for an honest discussion in the review. It was by doing this that appreciation grew of the fruitfulness of this experience. This may have been realized eventually but the review process brought it to the fore and the journal captured it all to help with the story. So in this worked example we have gone from using a journal to capturing an experience to review.[14]

Sharing with Someone

The various stories so far have included sharing the story with someone. In story 1 the stewardship campaigner talked to his wife, tried to talk to the Vicar, and talked to the Reader. It was not, however, until the pastoral care course that there was space to talk in a helpful way. In story 7 the narrator seems to have

---

13   F Bee and R Bee, *Facilitation Skills* (London: IPD, 1998) pp 167–171.
14   See also, R L Kinast, *Let Ministry Teach: A Guide to Theological Reflection* (Collegeville: Liturgical Press, 1996) pp 29–30.

come to some conclusions, but these then have to be discussed in a group, the church council. In story 8 there is a review in which each person can look back and state their reflections. This action of sharing with someone is part of the process of learning from experience and must not be neglected.

Some people have a prayer partner (as in story 8) or a spiritual director to help them think about their life. In looking back and learning from incidents in pastoral care it is important to have someone with whom to share. Incidents come up in our normal life, and if we become a part of a pastoral team (visiting, baptismal preparation, marriage preparation, bereavement visiting) it is important to have the opportunity to discuss those incidents that make an impression on us.[15]

The analysis of experience that is being used in this book can be done alone, but is much strengthened in talking over with someone. It is too easy to get the wrong end of the stick or become convinced that God wants us to do something. It is in talking it over and sharing with someone that real discernment can develop. In doing this we again will suggest a simple model.

If you visit for the church or are a part of a team it is important that you get an opportunity to talk over your critical incidents. The danger is that you are not listened to (as in story 1). There are some simple rules that can really help, and can be illustrated by a negative example. Imagine bringing back to the group an issue and this being the conversation:

A I found it really difficult talking to Mr X tonight. I think he had been drinking.
B You should have left, you cannot help people who are drunk.
A I do not think he was drunk.
B I remember visiting someone who was alcoholic. In the end I gave up. He would not go to AA.
A But I do not think that he is that bad, just a bit low.
B Well the Bible says 'Do not get drunk.' Do not forget that.
A Yes I know Paul says that.
B So, I can get you some information about AA. You could take it round next time you go.

I should imagine that A would feel quite frustrated by this. B has not really been listening and has been imposing his own experience and solution to a problem raised. If you begin to listen to conversations you will find that this is a common problem.

In listening to someone telling their incident, it is important not to impose your own views and solutions. Listen to the other person's story. Ask questions for clarification (this may be needed for you to grasp the situation) and look for opportunities the storyteller provides to go deeper. Look for hints of the real questions and concerns. If you can discuss these, then the person will really have been enabled in his or her ministry. This listening approach makes helping the other

15   See J Foskett and D Lyall, *Helping the Helpers: Supervision and Pastoral Care* (London: SPCK, 1988).

person tell their story and come to their own conclusions the aim of the meeting. Doing this in a partnership where one tells and the other helps, and then the process is reversed, can be a very fruitful approach. Talking through an incident with someone in this way strengthens and often clarifies the learning for all involved.

This chapter has looked at two linked activities in learning from experience. The first is keeping a journal. This in particular helps in capturing the experience and can be the basis for later reflection. Having done the analysis and reflection, sharing that with a partner or a supportive group can further enhance the learning. It is important to avoid indulging merely in navel gazing, and to make sure that reflection leads to action, the subject of the next chapter.

6
Acting on New Learning

The Epistle of James says, 'Do not just listen to his word...but put it into practice' (James 1.22). The model of learning that underlies the approach of this book is one that includes moving on to action. This chapter looks at the place of action.

A Model for Learning

Looking at critical incidents in the way envisaged in this book entails some action. The roots of the approach were in pilot training and industry and commerce. This has been applied to teaching, clinical practice and pastoral care because it can foster a climate of ongoing learning in ministry. Often we are naïve and think that having done the course we have learned and can be let loose. We come down to earth with a bump when we find that we do not have all the answers or skills we might need. Thus a more dynamic model of 'ongoing learning' is replacing the old model of 'get qualifications and minister.' This can be represented as follows:

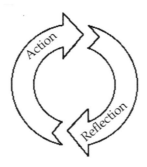

Critical incidents are those incidents that for some reason or another stick in our minds. They are the experience of raw action. The methods of analysis that we have recommended are ones that help in clarifying what happened and draw us into a reflective process of learning. This includes asking questions about what God is doing in these events. This leads on to further action.[16] Reflection is not an end in itself. It is supposed to lead back to action, so that the circle becomes a spiral.[17] The fact that this does not happen can be due to barriers that exist.

Barriers to Learning

If you find this model hard, it may simply be a question of understanding and practice. However, many of us have experiences that make some things difficult to do and even have to unlearn some things later in life.[18] When I was 12 I had to learn a poem by heart and recite it to the class. I was quite nervous about this and did not know very much about poetry. I chose a short poem and began to recite it. After one line the teacher stopped me, told me I was doing this wrong and asked me to start again. This happened at three different points. I felt humiliated and spent the next seven years avoiding having to do any sort of solo before a group of people. Not only were the feelings raw, but also the lesson I came away with was that I was no good before others and this would always lead to humiliation. Such experiences become barriers.

Other barriers can develop. It is easy not to distinguish between 'telling stories' and 'learning from experience.' It is easy to end up with a surfeit of anecdotes and a dearth of reflection and consideration about what might have been occurring. A good example of this from church life is the sort of conversations that take place when a minister leaves her/his post, both by the minister and the church and community. Effort is required to learn from that experience. Everyone might benefit from asking, 'What did we learn here?' 'What are we going to do?' These are key questions, if reflection is to feed back into a new experience. The history of some congregations, and ministers, would suggest that there are some major barriers to learning from experience and so history begins to repeat itself.

Previous experience, prejudices, snobberies, and downright false teaching can all be barriers to growth and progress. Why is it that so many church profiles want a minister who is aged 35, has a young family and who has 20 years of experience! Such criteria are impossible to fulfil. Critical, even peculiar, incidents can reveal these assumptions. Sometimes growth is through identifying these barriers and unlearning them. Thus the change in attitude can lead to radical new action. The lives of the saints are full of stories of this happening, the most dramatic example often being in conversion.

---

16   The diagram is after J Foskett and D Lyall, *Helping the Helpers: Supervision and Pastoral Care* (London: SPCK, 1988) p 8.
17   See L Green, *Let's Do Theology* (London: Mowbray, 1990).
18   See D Boud, R Cohen and D Walker (eds), *Using Experience for Learning* (Buckingham: SRHE/Open University Press, 1993) pp 73–86.

Types of Action

A simple action-reflection model is helpful as a starter since it is easy to grasp. The stories that we have told so far indicate a variety of actions.

- Story 1 was about changing attitudes. It might, however, have become a focus for improving supervision in the stewardship campaign. Who pastors the visitors? Perhaps the group sessions could have been not only about the aim—raising the level of giving—but also about the process—how this was gone about—and about caring for the visitors.
- Stories 2 and 3 were from the Bible and were about God's calling and a change of lifestyle.
- Story 4 dealt with coping with illness and how sometimes we have to change ourselves in the light of long-term illness.
- Story 5 was about how we are helped to deal with unresolvable disappointment in our lives.
- Story 6 led to a change in attitude in doing ministry and recognizing our shadow side.
- Story 7 was also about change. This time a change in one person's views resulted in action of raising the issue. Raising the issue led to the next action—a discussion in the church council. But it could have gone further, for national church policies have sometimes arisen from local initiatives.
- Story 8 was about worries at work. It turned out that these were about new responsibilities. What if they had been about ethical issues or company practice and policy? Again it is not impossible for reflection to lead to changes in practices. One of the early uses of critical incident analysis was in the production line, leading to greater efficiency. It can also be used to reflect on the place of people in production, which may raise questions of humanizing the process.

Thus action can be in a variety of ways from personal to corporate. It might lead to wider changes, both in the church and in society. This may lead to renewed effectiveness in pastoral care, but that cannot be divided from outreach in society and action in trying to change society. The demands of the kingdom are such that the wider horizons have to be considered in looking at experience and learning from it.

It may be that you find such suggestions of the wider dimensions to reflection uncomfortable. This in itself might be considered to be a critical incident and worthy of reflection. Working through our models might reveal attitudes to the relationship between the church and the world that are at variance with some of the assumptions behind what has been written in this chapter. That is fine; the important thing is to realize the differences. If you believe that the world is coming to an end soon and the role of the church is to 'snatch people from the fire' then much energy might be put into evangelism. That being so, what are you learning from your experience of outreach? It is fanatics who close their eyes, do not consider what they are doing, and redouble their efforts. What if you are into community development but the church is empty? 'It's not about bums on pews, but letting the kingdom grow in the community,' might be your approach. Fine— so what does your experience tell you about community and the role of a church in the community? There are plenty of examples of a search for spirituality and community in our society. How can a local church contribute to this quest?

These are all big questions. The suggestion of this book is twofold:

1. That critical incidents can reveal underlying attitudes which in turn may lead to asking big questions.
2. That all big answers need some sort of starting point and that the start has sometimes been the action of a few, thoughtful and reflective people working both locally and on wider policy.

Reflection without action stops growth and learning in this holistic model.

A Practical Suggestion

For effective action to take place, it is important to understand how the process of learning from experience works for you, perhaps by using some of the methods in this book. One way of doing this would be to turn this book into the basis for a learning partnership. This can be set up as follows:

1. Arrange with another person to meet once a month much as in story 8.
2. Agree to look at an incident in advance, using the methods outlined here.
3. Share with one another, helping each one in turn to develop his or her own learning without the other imposing a solution.
4. Keep a journal and write up the process of action and reflection.
5. Notice when this circle moves into a spiral and the whole thing begins to develop.
6. Set times for review so that this does not become a never-ending partnership but one that can grow and develop and end at the right time.
7. If this is surrounded with prayer and asks 'Where is God in this?' then the journal will also become a record of God's blessing and leading.

Action might sound like hard graft. With God at work there are always exciting unexpected possibilities.

7

Taking this Forward in Ministry

The 8 stories used so far have illustrated the use of critical incident analysis by individuals. It can also be used by groups to consider incidents and issues.

Story 9

For the first time, members of our church's young people's group had spent three days at a major national Christian festival. They had returned full of enthusiasm for the whole experience and eager to tell folk how good it had been. They were given a five-minute slot at the end of Sunday worship to tell the congregation about it. That evening, the Worship Group, of which I am the Convener, met. We decided to take time to describe our impressions of the young people's slot and the response to it, our own feelings and those of other people. We did this on our own and then wrote everything up on a flip chart. This raised a number of questions, which we also wrote on the flip chart. The questions were: Although we say that we value the young people in our church, is this really true? How can we find appropriate ways for them to contribute to leading the worship and the decision-making in our church? How can we incorporate people's experiences into the life of our church? What is the connection between what we do in our church and what God might be doing elsewhere? We agreed to each think further on these questions and come with responses to our next meeting. At the next meeting we decided that each of us on the Worship Group would attend a Youth Service/Event within the next six months and to invite two young people to join the Group with a view to reviewing the place of youth in our worship.

It is unlikely that one person working alone would have produced such a range of questions. By using all the perceptions and feelings from the different members of a group, the analysis had both greater variety and depth. The next stage might be to give all the members of the Worship Group the *Reflecting on the Incident* sheet outlined in chapter 4.

Some of the benefits of critical incident analysis are:

- It helps us to learn about ourselves.
- It has good biblical precedents.
- It places our stories within the Christian story.
- It is straightforward to apply.
- It can help us move from being 'victims' to 'learners.'
- It is used elsewhere, notably in the nursing and teaching professions.
- It is realistic—it helps one to see that some things can be redeemed and some cannot.

- It can be linked easily to theological reflection and thus the life and death of Jesus.
- It helps get behind the façade or presenting symptoms.
- It stops us being merely activist in our approach to ministry.
- It can be used for successes and failures, both great and small.
- It is a tool to help us grow, not a stick with which to beat ourselves.
- It facilitates skills in analysis and reflection.
- It can be used in a group for parish development.
- It can be used by anyone.

Its role in pastoral care is:

- To provide a framework for evaluating one's practice.
- To help us learn about our assumptions, biases and prejudices.
- To use our imagination in thinking of alternative ways of doing things.
- To enable us to identify areas for new learning.

At this point what is needed is for you to do some critical incident analysis for yourself. While it is important to understand the theory and method, reading about it does not mean that you can now do it. You do not become a mechanic through reading a car manual; it takes training and time, skill and experience. Although we believe critical incident analysis is easy to grasp, it takes time to get the full benefits just as it takes time to grow in wisdom. It would be fairly straight-forward to work through an experience using one of the methods in chapter four and to share it with someone. Remember that we have been saying that it is always important to talk your thoughts through with someone who can help you. Slightly more adventurous would be to follow the suggestion at the end of the last chapter. If you still want to read more, you could follow up the footnotes in this booklet. Particularly important are the books on theological reflection which has only been touched on in part in this booklet due to lack of space. The aim of all this is to help you grow in wisdom, and in the knowledge of God and yourself.